CHAPTER ONE

THE SEDUCTION OF MARTHA

This book is dedicated to the loves of my life my daughter Jennifer Ponce, my son Shawn Khalifa and Grandson Jackson Ponce.

It all started on a warm August night. Joe and Martha were nestled in a hidden cove on a beach in Venice, California. The date was August 17, 1987.

"God Martha, I don't know who you're holding out, for Christ's sake. You're seventeen, a God damn woman not a child. You walk around with tits as ripe as melons, screaming to bust out of that tight 'God Damn' tee shirt. Legs up to your arm pits; your shorts in a Melvin and the cheeks of your ass laughing at me—winking and teasing with your every motion. For Christ sake, I'm a man have pity. What are you saving it for anyway? You know, there was an article in Time Magazine a while back; it was all about a thirty year old prude who waited so long her cherry turned to stone.....that's right! Stone! It stopped up all her pee; she swelled up so big she couldn't

3

reach the bathroom door. She turned into a human piss balloon, exploded and all that remained was a river of pee and a pile of clothes. You tell me, what is the point is really."

Martha started to laugh, "Oh Joe, you really crack me up. Girls have two holes, one for fucking and having kids, the other for peeing. I swear to God Joe, you can be such a moron sometimes."

"Martha, please just hear me out, that's all I ask. Please! I love you. I wasn't put on this earth to hurt you. I want to share me with you. That must mean something. It is the one and only thing I have to offer right now".

"Joe, Martha cried. I know you mean well. I love you too, but I'm scared. My guide told me my destiny was to remain a virgin and become part of a crusade to save the world from self-destruction." Joe could feel his emotions begin to boil. It was those God Damn crystals again. Shit, he thought to himself, maybe Martha was becoming insane-possessed.

Not really trusting himself, he started in again.

"Martha I can't take this any longer. Those crystals are a game for Christ sake. Fuck, it's a wee gee board and you're letting it break us up, destroying our love. Oh Martha, where's your common sense, you're a smart girl don't let me down. I would not hurt you for the world. I want to play you gently, like a precious melody on a guitar. Strumming your every nerve until you burst into a symphony of pleasure, beyond anything you can imagine. Please come with me honey let me take you to heaven. Forget your make believe guide, throw your toys in the trash, and join me in life's greatest adventure."

Martha felt like a fool. Her Joe sat here before her so cute. She tingled every time he was close. She could not imagine life without him.

"Okay Joe, I am going to trust you. I'm putting myself in your hands, just take care of me right now, I am feeling so fragile". Joe could not believe his ears. The battle was finally won after all the months of begging and pleading. "Oh God", he thought to himself, Now that it was really going to happen he knew he had to take care to do everything just right. He just couldn't not blow this.

"Okay Joe, he said to himself, calm down, first things first. Set the mood, get relaxed. A six pack of beer would do the trick. Joe was reluctant to leave Martha alone, while he went after the beer; because dusk was starting to settle, he worried about the night creatures, street people, alcoholics, and drug addicts, who would be creeping out starting at dusk.

"Martha," Joe approached her carefully, trying not to upset the moment.

"I want to get some beer and I want you to come with me".

"Okay sure," Martha said and they started off on the short walk to his brother's apartment. The trip was made in silence, each deep in their own thoughts. Joe was secretly watching Martha, capturing the beauty of her long flowing hair as the soft twilight of the night illuminated it. She wore French cut shorts which left the cheeks of her ass exposed. He became mesmerized by their motion. The rise and fall of each cheek with every step she took. God he thought what a turn on, how anyone could be so voluptuous and vulnerable at the same time he did not know. He really did love her, he wanted to please her, and protect her. He wanted to keep her happy forever. He was going to make this the best night of her life.

After Joe and Martha returned to the beach, Martha approached the subject that had been on her mind since they had left.

"What about protection Joe?"

"Martha, Martha, Martha! Leave that up to me. I have it all under control; don't worry your pretty little head. Why, did you know that a man's penis is sometimes referred to as plumbing? Do you know why that is?" He rushed on,

"That is exactly how they work. We can turn them on and off anytime we want, just like a faucet. For instance, I turn it off while we're doing it and after it's over, I pull it out and turn it on again. My sperm goes into the sand and walla, no harm done, plain and simple, comprenda?"

"Yes." Martha sighed, "I hope you know what you're doing, and this isn't another piss balloon story."

"Trust me baby. You know I love ya."

"Do ya"?

"Sure Joe, sure".

After the second beer the tension began to ease and Joe and Martha laid back in each other's arms. Joe gazed into Martha's mist filled eyes, reaching his hand underneath her tee shirt. He began massaging her nipples with his fingertips. As they began to harden, Martha could feel an unexpected twinge of pleasure deep between her legs. She closed her eyes and became lost in the moment. Joe's other and spread her thighs and he began to gently rub her clitoris back and forth between his thumb and forefinger until she began to twitch and moan with uncontrollable pleasure.

As Martha's pleasure began to mount to heightened ecstasy, Joe gently parted her vagina and probed with two fingers until she was juicy and ripe for entering. Joe mounted her with his penis throbbing, and groin on the verge of explosion. Just as he began to enter her, like a slap in the face or ammonia shoved under your nose during a fainting spell, Martha was released from her moments of passion, by the sharp pungent odor of urine. At that moment the unsteady feet of a bum tripped unceremoniously over their entwined bodies. Martha jumped and screamed. Joe's partially inserted penis prematurely exploded, spilling semen between Martha's thighs and pubic area. This went unnoticed in her confusion and excitement.

Almost instantaneously, in the moonlit sky a new star was born….

"Oh," Martha exclaimed," Joe, I'm so sorry."

"Joe! Joe! It's alright, it's okay, really. I guess destiny can't be changed and my destiny is to remain a virgin forever"

"I swear, baby I'll make this up to you, I promise. It'll do better next time."

"I know Joe; now I'm incredibly tired.

Please just take me home. Okay"?

****

CHAPTER 11

HE'S BACK

That night Martha fell into a deep totally exhausted sleep, when she woke up the next day, she felt unusually happy. Her mother was sitting at the kitchen table, looking haggard after a night of way too many beers and cigarettes. Susan noticed some sort of a change in Martha, as she walked it to the kitchen, the atmosphere seemed to brighten. It was almost like a breath of fresh air, at once the grease splattered stove and the sticky counter tope became insignificant.

"Mom, how are ya doing," Martha inquired.

"Fine babe, real fine. You're a nice sight this morning. You know I guess I'm sort of missing you lately; you're growing up to fast. I can't believe you've grown to be such a lovely young lady just seems like yesterday I was burping you and changing your diapers. God! My baby has grown up. Sometimes, I feel like everything would be okay if I could just sit and rock you like I used to…. Brushing your hair from your eyes and talking and laughing about the same old things,-- The Three Little Pigs, and Disneyland. God, I miss those days probably too much."

Martha reached out and stroked her mother's hair.

"Oh mom," she said "If I could I would turn back time and crawl back into your lap again. I'd lay my head against your big boob pillows, we could sit and rock and rock. But mom, the time would pass again. What then? I'm the basket you're putting too many eggs in and it's suffocating me. Mom, you're not being fair to me or yourself. If you keep going the way you are, it's me who's going to miss you. Only difference is, you won't be here to talk about it."

Martha's mom recognized the truth in what she said. She shifted the mood resolving to make this a new day with a new beginning. She smiled at Martha and said, "I love you so much babe. You know something this is the first day of the rest of my life and it's going to be beautiful." Martha hugged her mom feeling the warmth that came from their strong bond of love.

The day was uneventful and routine. Martha walked the beach enjoying the laughter of the children on the playground. She sat for hours watching the waves as they gathered momentum exploding into cottony billows of foam and rolled to the shore. Even though the day was boring, there was a calming beauty about it. Not only did the ocean sparkle from the brilliant sunshine, everything had a bit of a sparkle. Martha could feel the freshness of the air in each breath she took.

That evening Martha sat in her room contemplating her crystal set. "Why not," she thought, I really believe in this. It's not a toy, I know this to be true, if I don't use the crystal's I will be betraying my own belief, and that would not be right. Martha began to meditate, then turned to her crystals which had already started in motion. She asked the standard question:

"Are you in the name of Jesus?" The crystal began to move spelling out slowly, I am Jesus." Martha's breath caught in here throat. That's ridiculous, she thought to herself. I must have read wrong. She repeated the question.

"Are you in the name of Jesus?" A very gentle voice answered,

"Child, don't be frightened, I am Jesus."

"You are?" she retorted, "You really are? I don't believe this I must be dreaming."

"No the soft comforting voice answered, you are not dreaming. You are a chosen one, my child. Do you remember your guide told you that you would be part of a crusade to save mankind? Well, you are to be the mother of the child Jessell. She will be the second coming of Christ.

"She?" "I thought Jesus was a man."

"There is no sex in heaven when we enter the Earth's realm, we must assume a life form, Male or female, it makes no difference."

Martha started to shake her head back and forth.

"This can't be happening," she muttered I'm standing here having a conversation with God. Right, I'm the chosen one. I'm insane, right it runs in the family." Mom said grandma went insane, mom had her moments too. Now it's my turn."

"Calm down, little one, Christ said, it's alright relax and listen to me. At this very moment, as we speak your body houses the most precious possession the Earth will have known. My daughter Jessell."

I don't understand. Why me? I not good I make mistakes and lots of them. Here is another good one, do you know I have never stepped foot into a church."

"Of course, I know don't forget I know everything", God retorted.

"First of all you are human and you were designed to make mistakes. Let me put it to you this way, the human race is the prototype in my divine creation. You make mistakes because I made a mistake. If I can accept that why can't you."

Martha started to understand. "Yeah, that makes sense, Martha said.

"Is that going to be part of the crusade?" She asked.

"Yes a small part but definitely a part. Please let me continue a moment," God said, "So you have never been to church. Well, there are good people who go to church, and there are bad people who go to church. Not to point fingers or name names but James Town did exist and in the name of Jesus, Reverend Jerry Falwell and the Baker's continue to preach and receive support. I'm not saying churches are bad, no they are good very good a tool actually. Like any other tool it becomes nonfunctional if not used properly. Bottom line is churches are a convenience not a necessity.

"You have a beautiful clean soul Martha, always remember that. Now I must leave you with a message. You are a human being and nothing can change that. You are more than likely going to experience a tragedy in your life time. Tragedy is only as significant as you let it become. Some people live their lives in fear, bracing themselves for the next blows, these people always get hurt the hardest. Life is a gift. Live it, love it, and enjoy it. There is beauty everywhere in everything. Search for it and find it. Even tragedy has beauty, if it happens feel it, accept it and let it pass. I love you Martha. You will have peace and happiness for all eternity. Martha don't use the crystals anymore. They are potentially dangerous, evil spirits from beyond the grave, have a field day with types of mediums like these. Goodbye my child. I'll see you in 29 years, 9 months, 8 hours and 32 seconds. Don't forget talk to me as often as you like I'll always be listening.

******

CHAPTER III

MOM'S HOME

Joe waved at Martha from across the room as he entered the café. It was a small cozy coffee shop off the beach called the "Side Walk Café." The place was jam packed and overcrowded as usual.

Joe kept bumping into people as he made his way across the room. He was more than a little nervous after receiving a cryptic phone call. He hadn't even gotten seated before Martha, started to burst forth with the news.

"Hey, wait a minute! Let me sit down. Now, what did you say? Tell me again I could not hear you."

She began again, slowly and deliberately.

"Joe, I'm pregnant, Joe." He started to feel the color drain from his face. The overwhelming wave of nausea began to overcome him. Martha immediately realized her error in blurting out her news, as Joe's face started to contort. She raced forward trying to undo the damage.

"Oh no Joe, it's not what you thinks. I'm still a virgin. You are the only person I have ever let touch me like that. Remember Virgin Mary was baby Jesus's Mother and Joseph was the father, but they never had sex." Joe felt like he was on an emotional roller coaster. What the hell was this girl saying? Joe just sat for a moment, looking at her in utter disbelief. His eyes started to water a little as began to blink the enormous headache he felt coming on.

"Hold the phone a minute! You mean to tell me you think you're Virgin Martha, the snicker turning into a laugh. Virgin Martha, he began to laugh uncontrollably, tears streaming down his face. The more he laughed the louder he got and at some point, he was slapping his knee.

Martha felt like crawling under the table. The polite glances of the other diners had turned to open mouthed gaping stares. Feeling beyond the ultimate humiliation, Martha's instincts overcame her. With reflect motion she reached for her glass of water and hurled it into Joe's laughing face. Making matters worse. Instantly realizing with horror what she had done, Martha could only think of one thing, escape. She bolted for the door blindly pushing people and chairs out of her way. She didn't stop running until she was at the water's edge. She just sat down, folded hands and head in her lap and started sobbing oblivious to anything or anybody around her.

Joe started to sober the instant the cold water hit his face. As he watched Martha running toward the beach, he knew he couldn't leave her alone. He had to go after her. Joe's natural good humor surfaced as he made his exit, he turned and faced the crowd, pivoting around he took several bows and did a little side shuffle waving as he went out the door. He spotted Martha on the beach, her head still down and her shoulders moving up and down in rhythm with her sobs. As he approached she looked up and her tear stained face erased all humor from the situation. He felt an overwhelming desire to cradle her in his arms. Joe reached out and as they embraced, he felt a rush of deep affection. His adolescent feelings of like and desire instantaneously matured into a deep founded love. Unaware of the transition they continued to embrace until they felt comfortable enough to more apart.

"Martha I'm sorry, it was just too much to take at once. I guess I sort of cracked or something." Martha shyly smiled still a little embarrassed.

"No it's my fault. I realize how ridiculous I must have sounded. I wouldn't have believed me either."

"Martha I know you. You are too gullible and trusting, but you're not crazy. I can't comprehend what you are saying, but I want you to know I'm here and I will stand by you whatever it is."

"Thanks Joe, that's is all I want and need. I could never ask for anymore."

Martha's mother was pleasantly surprised when she came home from work and found the kids had cold beer and hot pizza waiting for her.

"Hey you guy's what's the occasion? You just win a million dollars on the lottery and you came to break the news."

"No mom, nothing like that. It's just we haven't seen much of you lately and we thought we'd hang around awhile. You know, shoot the breeze and maybe mess around a little."

"Sounds fishy, but I like it."

Martha, her mom, and Joe had always has a mutually friendly relationship. Joe could talk to Martha's mom easier than he could his own. Joe got a twinkle in his eye.

"Hey Mrs. P", he said "losing a little weight lately……."you're starting to look real good." He grabbed her hips, shaking them back and forth, yelled "Shake that booty, WOW. Wild and crazy woman. What do you think of younger men?"

"Oh, get out of here Joe, Martha's mom blushed. You're such a moron sometimes."

As the evening progressed, they found themselves laying around the living room, laughing, joking and drinking beer. Martha turned to her mom, her face suddenly sober.

"Mom, I've got to tell you something."

"Oh no here it comes" she said, beginning to feel leery again. Remembering her mistake with Joe, Martha started at the beginning. Conveniently forgetting to mention the mishap on the beach, she talked until the whole story was out.

Joe looked at Martha's mom intently. She, in turn, focused her attention on him.

"Joe, I know how you must feel. I must admit I'm a little confused myself. I've listened to what Martha has said and I want you to know I'm her biggest fan. I believe in what she says and does 100%. There is a world that we cannot see, but we know it exists. For example, electrons flow and frequencies are transmitted, we use them every day. Three hundred years ago if someone were to tell you about them you'd probably think they were making up a fairy tale. Speaking of fairy tales some of the things in the Bible, if you were to really think about them would defy common sense and reason. A man, all by himself builds a boat—

not a ship, that houses every kind of animal species, which survives through horrendous floods. Is this a space ship from alien creatures, who knows? A lady turns and looks at a city and she turns to salt. Was this an alien weapon that disintegrated the woman? I wonder if it was iodized or un-iodized salt. Okay that was stupid, let me think. Yes, and there was Mary, she become the mother of Jesus and Joseph is the father—and she was still a virgin. All of what I am saying is both morally and socially accepted. Is it any stranger than what Martha is telling us? I'm sorry I am babbling aren't I."

"No, No, Mrs. P...You're doing fine. It sort of makes sense really."

"Mom, Martha began, I'm happy and I want us all to be happy. I love you guy's. I want you to feel what I'm feeling. I want you to share in my glorious fortune. Oh God, you guys, I want to run, dance, sing, and scream from the roof tops. Oh Jesus, it all feels so right and good." She hugged herself around the waist, turned around on her heels and smiling she looked up at the sky, seeing far, far, beyond the stars and darkness of the night.

****

CHAPTER IV

SORRY WRONG NUMBER

As Martha approached the desk at the Kaiser clinic, a woman with a petite, cute little figure was bent over a computer key board tying intently. Martha stood patiently waiting to be noticed.

"Hey you bitch, a man with five o'clock shadow and yellow caked teeth, spat viciously. He began impatiently pounding his fist on the desk.

"Hey, you fish ass", he started again. As she calmly turned, Martha noted the sharp contrast between her figure and face. Her face was aged with sagging skin and bagging eye lids.

"Oh, beg pardon, I meant fish face. I want help NOW!"

"Could I please have your name?"

"yeah, you can have my name. My name is Henry. Fuck me I the ass and your dead." As he spat forth the words, his mouth worked back and forth uncontrollably.

"You people are mother fucking lying sons of bitches." He turned his narrowed, slightly yellowed eyes to the other patients in the waiting room, and began to sing a crazed song to the tune of the Bottle Hymn of the Republic.

"I am fucking dying and without trying, these sons of a bitches give me a bill for a pill, that turns my piss blue, and when I say achoo, I vomit up red. So with my white head, they've me into the United States flag. Old fags, like old flags never die, they just fade, fade away. Let's hear it for the flag, Yea, Yea, Y

ea."

He turned and hit the desk again, his energy diminishing. His ankles and knees gave out at the same time as he sank to the floor. His chin sharply hit the edge of the desk snapping his head back in a grotesque motion. A team of professionally trained personnel came to his aid. Martha noted that he must have recently lost a tremendous amount to weight. His belt was past the last hole and was wound around itself and secured into his ill-fitting pants.

"Miss, may I help you?" Martha's attention was redirected toward the receptionist.

"I'm here for a pregnancy examination."

"Write your name at the bottom of that list, fill out these forms and return them to me."

"Wow! I wonder what that was all about, Joe asked, as Martha retuned to the seat next to him. He looked like he was on crack or cocaine. Did you see his mouth?

"Yeah, reminds me of the return of the living dead."

Martha filled out the questionnaire and returned it to the receptionist.

"Please take your seat and your name will be called when it's your turn."

"What time is your appointment? 2:30? Shit, it's 4:00 now," Joe complained. "I wish we could leave. This place gives me the creeps."

"We can't. This appointment took me two months to get."

Joe shifted his buns irritably in his seat.

"Joe, you go for a walk, get a soda across the street or something. You don't have to sit with me. I'll be going in pretty soon, anyway."

"You sure you don't mind?"

"Na, I will feel better."

"OK babe, see you in a few. I got to get some fresh air. I won't take too long."

The nurse stuck her head in the door.

"Maria Sanchez", she called. The woman sitting several seats down from Martha flinched as a spasm of pain overtook her.

"I am Maria Sanchez, "she managed to gasp out.

"Please follow me you are next."

Maria, slightly bent in pain pushed her baby stroller to the door.

"I am sorry, you can't bring the baby in."

"I no leave alone. No good."

"I'm sorry, it's against policy."

"It hurt so, help Maria begged." Martha approached and lightly touched her shoulder. "I'll watch your baby." She offered.

"You strange, I no know," she said brokenly. The nurse's impatience was surfacing.

"Miss, you'll have to find someone to watch your baby, then you can come back."

"I all alone, Maria said weekly as she turned to push her baby though the door, still bent in pain.

"Martha Prescott."

"Yes."

"Please follow me." They passed through two double doors, entering into a hallway with half a dozen doors on each side, they opened into color coded cubicles.

"Go to the blue room second to the right, remove your cloths and put on the gown at the end of the examining table."

Martha closed the door and began to remove her tee shirt and jeans. She ran her hands across her slightly swelled stomach, stroking it gently with loving caresses. She sat at the end of the examining table patiently waiting for the arrival of the doctor. When she was surveying the various disinfectants and examining utensils, the doctor entered, causing her to jump slightly.

"Well, young lady, I hope congratulations are in order because I see that the blood tests are back, and you're at least two months pregnant." Martha squealed with delight.

"I knew it, I knew it." She sang joyously throwing her arms around the doctor and giving him a bear hug. The doctor colored slightly.

"It's always a refreshing change to bring news when it's good. Now be a good girl, scoot back, put your legs up in the stirrups, and then bring your bottom to the edge of the table."

Seeing Martha's hesitation and noting her age, he asked,

"Are you scared?"

"A little. I've never been examined before."

"Well relax, and do what I say and I promise it'll be over with before you know it."

Martha took several deep breaths and then laid back, clenching her teeth preparing for the worse. As he bent his dirty, greasy looking head and began applying lotion to his hands, a realization hit Martha. Why wasn't he supposed to have a nurse in here? And, he doesn't have gloves on! Just as she was about to object, he unceremoniously thrust two fingers into her pelvis with one swift movement, she jumped from the table. Hands on hips she demanded irately,

"You're supposed to have a nurse in here and gloves on. What are you---some sort of pervert or something?"

The doctor couldn't reply immediately to her accusations. He was too busy trying to rationalize what he had just felt.

"Hey, what is this?" he blurted, "You're still a virgin." He opened the door and yelled to the nurse.

"We need another blood sample, somethings screwy. Get back on the table, I need to examine you. There appears to be some sort of deformity and unless you cooperate, I won't be able to help you.

"Not on your life brother." Martha said as she sprang for the door, leaping out of the doctor's way she cleared the door and was through the reception rooms in a split second. She flew down the stops, hurling herself directly into Joe's arms.

"Oh Joe, thank God that was awful, just awful."

"What happened Babe? You're trembling. Hey, don't those hospital gowns have the back open?" Martha gasped and reached for her backside.

"Oh Joe, quick get behind me."

They made their way to Martha's mom's car like a pair of Siamese twins. As soon as they were sheltered safely in the car they burst into hysterical laughter.

****

CHAPTER V

Martha's beauty developed into an enchanting radiance as her inner peace grew united with the baby's embryo. The months passed quickly and the delivery time was fast approaching. Joe contemplated Martha out of the side of his eyes. They were driving along the Southern California coast on a bright, sunny, Saturday afternoon.

Her strange convictions of the subject of marriage perplexed him. She felt the marriage certificate and ceremony, a mockery of the natural phenomena which exists during the union of two people into the state of one being. She believed signing contracts and making promises opened avenues that would allow something to be broken. Once something is broken, it becomes weaker. The more it's broken the weaker it becomes and just as it exists, it can also be non-existent. He never expected this attitude from her. She did once tell him that she never lent money. If someone asked her and she decided to give it to them, she didn't expect to get it back. That way, if they did give it back, it was a plus and if they didn't she didn't expect it anyway; therefore, she didn't risk losing a friend.

"Okay, let me approach this from another direction," Martha said, breaking the silence.

"Say I promise to make you an apple pie, and after working hard all day that apple pie is all you can think about on the way home. Your stomach is growling, your pallet is ready for you to sink your teeth into the tantalizing, succulent, texture of freshly tart apple slices. The brown sugar and butter topping oozing through to the crust, which is perfectly crisp and fluffy. You enter the kitchen. You yell out,

"I'm home". You look around the kitchen. Your eyes narrow in disbelief, the apples are still in the fruit basket. From that moment on you'll associate that feeling of disappointment and me. On the other hand, if you come home from work not expecting an apple pie. As you enter the kitchen, your nostrils flare to the aroma of freshly baked pie, from that moment on your surprised happiness will be associated with me."

"I don't want you to make promises you can't keep." Joe said.

"Joe, you're still missing the point. It's not that It can't exist; don't expect anything and you won't be disappointed. Our love is our reward. For me-that's enough."

"Tell me how you honestly feel, Joe."

"Well I never really gave any of this much thought. It all kind of took me by surprise. I feel we've exhausted this conversation. I promise to support your convictions." John said seriously and continued with,

"All right my love", he said with a grin and a wink, "your wish is my command."

They took advantage of a red light and as their lips met, the warm flow of mutual love and affection overtook them, sending little sparks of passion through their blood streams, and causing their hearts to flutter.

That day, Mother Nature's mission was to prepare the birth place of the baby Jesell. She gently blew erasing all the smog, she cried tears of joy, cleansing the land, then smiled brightly, radiating warmth. Her duties competed all the heavens joined her rejoicing.

Martha and Joe were passing Doheny State Part just as Martha instinctively knew that Jesell's arrival, within minutes was imminent. The spirits of goodness were already in motion. They guided Joe and Martha skillfully through each step of the birth.

Just as a full moon upsets the natural balances of the unstructured energies, causing irrational and unusual behaviors the birth of Jessell brought harmony, enlightening the soul of mankind. Love and happiness were in the air, exposing the world to raw unpretentious splendor.

Through the night Martha, Joe and baby Jesell rested comfortable. The baby Jesell was safely secured in a barbecue pit lined with fresh newspapers and wrapped in clean blankets. In faraway places three very wise women had a vision. They witnessed heavenly lights carrying an infant through a maze of brilliance. The infant burst forth ascending into an intermediate suspension and entering a calm darkness, suddenly she was thrust into a realm of intimate feelings and being.

They heard the heavenly trumpets hale the lords for the baby Jesell was born. They traveled from three directions, following the bright southern star; one drove a car, one flew a plane, and the other rode a motorcycle. As they arrived   bearing gifts they fell to their knees praising Jesell to the highest. One brought a car seat so the baby could travel safely throughout her infancy. Also, she bear a set of keys to a new Chevy so Martha and Joe could have a safe car to house the new car seat. The second wise woman brought a new baby stroller so that baby Jesell could be strolled from place to place comfortably throughout her infancy. Also, she presented a set of keys to a brand new, completely furnished security condo in Marina Del Rey, so that baby Jesell could always be strolled into a safe home. The third wise woman brought a year's supply of pampers so that baby Jesells bottom would be dry. Also, she brought a set of keys to fit into a brand new MacDonald's on Lincoln Boulevard, so that Martha and Joe could make a substantial living. This way the baby's needs would be taken care of from both ends.

****

CHAPTER V1

Jesell laying in her crib, closed her eyes and journeyed home. She traveled deep within herself. At the sight of the first light she felt a great relief and called to Jesus, they were one in heaven but not on earth.

"Oh Jesell you're home. Their energies melded into one as they embraced. Their feelings were naturally transmitted.

"Your heart is hurting."

"Oh Father, I can't stand to see you hurt, for I know the pains and frustrations. Oh Jesus, there is so much to do. I don't know where to start. There is disease everywhere. I'm not talking about bodily diseases. Their souls are rotting and decaying."

"Father always regretted giving up on the fallen angels. He felt if he had invested a little more time he could have saved them. The earthling's souls have far surpassed theirs."

"What are we going to do? We need his infinite wisdom."

"Oh, my child I feel our worry. In my hind sight I now realize my mistake in giving them free will. I guess I'll have to rework the system."

Both Jesus and Jesell felt shock and dismay.

"Oh no, please don't take their free will away. You might as well condemn them all to hell. All those beautiful white souls and the souls of the children. The beautiful pearl blue of the wizened older souls. Please, it's not fair to punish them all."

"I understand your empathy, but the situation is becoming out of control. There are too many black souls; if this continues the divine creation could be affected. I'm sorry my daughter, I must bring you home." Jesus and Jesell spirits cried. A sudden comfort overtook them, as Mary entered them sweetly and instantly their troubled spirits were soothed.

"In my love there is hope. Let me show you the way, let me be your guide." Christ faded away giving Mary the final decision, for they are one. Jesus, Mary and Jesell exchanged thoughts.

"The ten commandments are obsolete. You know Father would not condemn a souls to eternal damnation because they skipped church on Sunday and went to the beach, and there are so many to add:

1. Thou shall not gorge yourself on food and then make yourself throw up.
2. Thou shall not solicit sex from minors.
3. Thou shall not use syringes to inject illegal drugs.
4. Thou shall not sell drugs to children."

"Hey wait, your heading in the wrong direction. All of your commandments have don'ts. There should be no don'ts. First we teach them hell. We are the ones that condemned them in the first place, if we didn't teach them hell, it would not exist."

"You've got something. We've gone about this the wrong way. You're right we have made laws that scare and threaten them into being good; after goodness they find God and achieve eternal happiness.

"That's ass backwards. First we teach them happiness and love, after a person has that they just naturally become good and that leads them directly to God." They began brainstorming "Almost everything that's fun if evil. Let's reverse that, evil spelled backwards is live. Let's make it fun to live. Stimulate pleasure centers by enhancing the gifts of Mother Nature. We'll use the same tactics as the Prince of the Spirit of Darkness by going through the back door. Let's put Disneyland in their souls and take the drugs out of their veins.

"We're on a roll here, we're onto something. The apostles could be artists. We'll penetrate the media. We could enter their subconscious during commercial with unrecognizable messages."

"Here's a good one. Create new instruments. For instance one will blend in perfectly with heavy metal. The kids will be drinking beer, smoking dope or taking some kind of drug. Their transmitting cells will be firing slower or faster than normal 72 millivolts, with their timing being out of sync. The beat of the message will penetrate their brains easily. Before they know what hit them, they'll be ours. As they travel through this life transitioning from their ancestors Adam and Eve to their spiritual beings, Jesus and Mary, they must be cleansed. White represents purity and the process will be repeated until it is achieved.

Jesell's grave depression was lifted. Their love united Jesell left, there were no goodbyes, for they lived within her.

"Oh my darling I see you're awake. Ah, come to grandma," Susan Prescott said as she lifted little Jesell from her crib. She sat and cradled Jesell, and as always, she was overwhelmed by her beauty. She was a delicate blend of all the best features, from all nationalities. Her hair was light brown with golden highlights. It swirled and framed her heart shaped face in luminous Shirley Temple like curls. Her large eyes were almond shaped, their color, hazel with little flecks of emerald green, her best feature, if she had a best because she was put together so perfectly was said to be her eyes. Her long, thick black lashes fringed her eyes like strands of silk. Susan sang softly in a pretty little voice.

"Ma Ma's little baby loves shortening, shortening, Ma Ma's little baby loves shortening bread. Call up the doctor, the doctor said feed them babies shortening bread."

"You have a beautiful voice, Grandma." Susan gasped in shock.

"I said you have a beautiful voice." Susan squealed in delight, hugging Jesell to her breast.

Jesell was slightly over a year old ad had never uttered a word.

"Oh my darling! You can talk. I can't believe my ears."

"Sure, I've always been able to talk."

"Then why haven't you?"

"I've never had anything to say until now."

"Oh God, this is wonderful. Talk to me—tell me everything."

"Well, I think you're beautiful; I love to cuddle in your lap. I like it so when mom and dad bring me here. I like the way your house smells, I like the way you smell.

"Oh Jesell baby, I love you so much." She hugged her lovingly with admiration shining in her eyes.

"I love you too, Grandma."

"What do you say, let's sit by the pool and drink a lemonade."

"Sure." Said Jesell as she jumped from her lap and ran to the door. Unlike talking, Jesell had never crawled, she had been walking since she was three months old.

As they were lulling around in the back yard, Susan watched as Jesell studied the intricate design of a butterfly, resting on a rose petal.

"It marvels me when I see heaven on earth."

"Jesell, what's it like?"

"Oh Grandma, it's wonderful, let's see, heaven consists of feelings. Take how you feel when someone says you're beautiful, or someone you love kisses you, or you're eating your favorite food. You're embraced in love, you're given birth, just won a million dollars, your wedding day, and pride in yourself or a loved one. If you take everything that makes you feel happy and multiply that feeling many times over, it would still not feel as good as heaven. You can only take your love with you, and as you leave behind the material things of this earth.

When you return home and the realization of who your spirit is and the overwhelming love igniting the reality, that you are still you and continue to live without pain and the opportunity to continue to learn and grow. Reaching the potential that is uniquely yours. We are one on earth but not in heaven.
"Why does heaven feel so good?"
"First of all, it's a great accomplishment to achieve the level of goodness to be accepted as part of the spirit. That sounds awfully hard. Actually for some it takes a life time but for others it happens instantaneously. Then there are the lucky few who are gifted at birth with goodness. There are usually borderline angels

who have a little more to prove or accomplish before making the transition. Heaven is pure love and knowledge living in a world where the only emotion is love is unbelievable. On earth people strive to be recognized, they want to be special that part does not go away in heaven, the only difference is that we are all one, and all special."

"You see we work with infinite numbers of creations. Christ is a supreme being, supreme but also a being. When a being exits he can never cease to exist. Just as a baby transforms to an aged person, one form will transform into another form."

 "I understand water to ice and can accept a world of unseen energies, but it's really hard for me to accept once something is dead it still exists, If I eat a hamburger and shit it out and it fertilized a plant, that poor cow is still dead.

That plant dies and could fertilized another plant or because it's organic, turns into oil, or maybe a diamond, which is inanimate. That's an evolution that evolves into an organic or an object. Diamonds don't decompose.

"No but diamonds bring emotion. It's a rare gem loved and cherished. A person who presents you with a diamond is saying love."

Jesell, did not know how to explain DNA and the historical links to the transition to the humane embryo and the spirit that chose to carry on the chain of events, depicted by relationships between the various generations, and keep the facts simple enough for her grandma to understand and digest. The simplistic nature of the reality was far from the capability of the human brain to comprehend. The mysteries of life will be understood by the transition from living housed in a body to the spirit housed in the universe.

The power of knowledge is determined by the level of transmission, is it gifted by the conditions of each individual life or it is earned as transcended by the level of spiritual achievement. We are all linked by our choices before and after birth. The beauty of an infant, is the awareness of the spiritual world it has just left. The new spirit is a direct link to its ancestry and as its parents love and nurturing is administered and as it grows it begins to separate from the spiritual choices of achievement mapped out and predestined. Freewill plays a great deal in the victory of triumphing over the bodily conflicts when reaching and triumphing over the predetermined destiny and attainment.

Jesell loved her grandmother so much she reached out and held her hand and simply stated,

"What you lose in this world you gain tenfold in heaven." You have a color an aura when all color turns to white, when our aura stabilized the light we are complete.

White light is made up of all the colors of light. Sunlight contains all the colors of light in a continuous spectrum. A prism may separate the colors and produce a rainbow. Every color has its own wavelength. In the visual spectrum of light, the color violet has the longest wavelengths and lowest frequency, followed by blue. These colors travel the farthest; this is the reason Mountains appear blue from a distance. Red is the highest frequency color, and it has the shortest wavelength of the visual spectrum. Visible light is only a small section of the full electromagnetic spectrum, which includes X-rays and radio waves as well.

Black is the darkest color, the result of the absence or complete absorption of light. Like white and grey, it is an achromatic color, literally a color without hue. It is one of the four primary colors in the CMYK color model, along with cyan, yellow, and magenta, used in color printing to produce all the other colors. Black is often used to represent darkness; it is the symbolic opposite of white (or brightness).

Black was one of the first colors used by artists in neolithic cave paintings. In the 14th century, it began to be worn by royalty, the clergy, judges and government officials in much of Europe. It became the color worn by English romantic poets, businessmen and statesmen in the 19th century, and a high fashion color in the 20th century.[2]

In the Roman Empire, it became the color of mourning, and over the centuries it was frequently associated with death, evil, witches and magic. According to surveys in Europe and North America, it is the color most commonly associated with mourning, the end, secrets, magic, force, violence, evil, and elegance.

In essence the absence of light caused by the Aura of hate and guilt produces the aura of black or evil while the light of the colors of love and forgiveness produces and Aura of love and goodness.

There is no water in heaven. All things evolve. When Christ created the earth, it did not take seven days, it took billions of years of evolution. Adam and Eve evolved from mutated microscopic creatures. The bible was written to give guidance and substance to life. It is full of parables and myths. How life was created and evolution would be too mind boggling for the inferior human brain to absorb. Even Einstein only kissed the surface.

"All things are created on different levels. The human, the highest creator on earth, is the lowest in heaven. Have you ever given thought to who Christ, Christ is or who is the Christ of Christs Christ?

"When you leave this life, your actually born into another whelm, your soul is the embryo your body the womb." Your living body battles your living soul, they are at odds and when they come together there is peace. If you leave this earth at peace this is the way you enter heaven.

****

CHAPTER VII

Jesell went to different churches headed by preachers, Rabbis and priests who were predestined for heaven. At first they were naturally shocked when they found themselves in deep conversations on theology with a five year old child. Jesell had an aura of infinite wisdom. Some would react with their backs against the wall and others would listen in awe. She didn't leave them until there were at least questioning their individual beliefs.

"Turn your churches into a school, medical center, teen entertainment center a home for the homeless, a restaurant to feed the poor and needy, rehabilitation center for drug addicts and alcoholics, or a day care center. Provide a free service to society," Jesell lectured,

"Open up your minds, I want to share with you a concept that's designed to change the world. This is the hottest thing since the invention of the zipper. Throw your bible away, it's been obsoleted—we're, as a society, being sucked in the predictions from the books of Revelations. We need to change direction by 180 degreees. The human race has become emotionally retarded, self-destructive and indulgent.

Take your parishioners back to nature; teach them to slow down. Send out flyers and meet them on a pristine beach next Sunday. These people are poor, they work hard all week, most of their jobs are routine and boring; their kids get sick, they must keep up the work at home, it's again routine and sometimes unrewarding. They go to sleep exhausted and wake up tired. Most of their recreation time is spent on the computer or other electronic devices or watching movies and TV shows that reinforce violence. The news is full of social injustice, corruption and the doom of disease and destruction. Put them in a fresh environment, teach them how to relax. Separate the children from the adults, let the young adults supervise the children at play, while the adults get to know each other; encourage communication. Invite them to share stories of any happy experience they have experienced surprisingly enough there will be many. We want to stimulate friendship and develop affection. Teach them to listen and meditate.

Bring the children and parents together to sing and to play. This will lead to an environment that cares, it stimulates empathy for your fellow man. It's like getting your feet wet before you swim. It's the plunge to eternal happiness. There are a few things that might surprise you about Christ. Two things he cherishes are laughter and rock and roll. You know the old saying the good die young; stop and think about how many rock and roll singers are killed in airplanes. One might argue that this is due to the amount of time they must commute and statistics but I believe that God is taking back what is only leant to us.

****

CHAPTER VIII

In the heart of LA there is a bleak, run-down, overcrowded apartment building in one of the apartments sat little Peter. He felt lost and alone as he contemplated his father from a lumpy soiled overstuffed chair. He sank as far back in the grimy cushions as he could, trying to go unnoticed. His father was wearing his traditional shabby blue jeans, they were so tight the impressions of his knees and private parts had worn the material thin and frayed. Peter watches as he raised his cigarettes to his lips and took and unhealthy drag, exhaled coughing at the same time.

Why can't he like me Peter thought, remembering a day many weeks before when he had been playing in his parents bed room and had picked up his mother's lip stick. He opened it up and smelled a faint reminder of his mother's gentle touch came from the smell.

He applied some to his lips in the same fashion he'd seen her use. Enjoying the moist contact he looked in the mirror and found pleasure in the transformation the bright color brought to his image. He picked up the blush and began to create and experiment, enjoying the escape into a fairy land, as he became the beautiful princess. He found a delicate lacy slip he put it on and twirled and swirled around, imagining little furry creatures in fields of blossoms waltzing with him.

His father's gruff voice, woke him rudely from his dreams.

"You God damn little faggot, get out of my sight before I kill you." Tears immediately welled up in Peter's eyes as he slid his way past his father and ran to his room. The deadly silence was broken when his mother came home from work and his father started in on her.

"That kids enough to make me puke, dancing around like a little Nancy. It's your fault you should have let me beat him up when he was a baby, knock some sense into his head, toughen him up."

"Come on George it's no one's fault, these things happen. We'll just have to make the best of the way things are.

"That's easy for you to say you don't have to introduce your son the guys, and say what. Hey you guy's this is my little fruit son, aint he cute. No, no way, keep the little shit out of my way. I'm warning you I don't trust myself. I can't stand the sight of him. I'll kill him, I swear to God, I will."

Peter laid on his bed and listened as his father rambled on and on.

"Nigger, fagot, no good sissy, word after work entering his subconscious reinforcing the realization of who Peter is, as he fell into a troubled sleep.

As the years passed, Jesell blossomed into a raving beauty. She was said to be beautiful both inside and out. The natural phenomena of her ravishing beauty drew people to her with raw animal magnetism. She was making progress but it was just not enough. It was like counting grains of sand on a mile square of beach, and she was up to 5,729,352.

On a very sunny afternoon very close to her thirteenth birthday she was strolling in a desolate wooded area in the outskirts of Malibu Canyon. As Jesell started to round a blind corner obstructed by a massive rock formation she became witness to a very gruesome scene.

A group of teenage children were surrounding a black youth who was crouched and groveling on the ground. A few of them held pieces of shredded clothing, which they had apparently stripped from him. Martha noted that all the children wore tight fitting surgical gloves. One oversized bully grabbed the boy's ass and held it air born. Two others pinned his hands outstretched in front of him. Another thrust the open end of a large wine bottle into his anus. The scream he let out was blood curdling.

"Ya like it your black bastard, fagot. Shit get the dog, this suckers God Damn asshole is as big, black and ugly as his fucking face. Look at it, his mother is pettier than this." He pulled the bottle brutally out and thrust it back in with muscled force. As the violent rap continued the soft delicate tissue of the victim's anus became torn and he was bleeding profusely. A second lad had begun dry pumping a large mixed pedigree dog.

"Let's see if doggies get aids." As he started to direct the dogs erect penis to the wounded anus, Jesell reached the group. The energy of her spirit immediately began conflicting with their spirits of evil. The superior quality of her energy posed such a threat that they immediately retreated, causing the youths to cower in fear. Backing away they broke into frenzied runs, stumbling and falling into each other as they clumsily made their escape.

Jasell reached fo the boy, touching him lightly on the shoulder. As her flesh came into contact with his, the wounds were healed; old scares were erased; disease was driven from his body and his soul was cleansed.

He looked up and as their eyes met he felt mesmerized.

"Who are you?"

"I'm Peter."

"Well Petey, it's nice to meet you." Jesell said as she extended her hand.

"It's sure good to meet you, you saved my life. What's happening to me?"

"I feel wonderful, there is no more pain. This is too good to be true."

"Hey, it is true just relax a moment. You've just been through a big ordeal."

"Oh, I feel so wonderful, liberated."

"Peter you are wonderful."

"No, No, I'm not."

"What do you mean?"

"I'm a misfit an embarrassment to my family and friends. I have strange feelings that are different than everybody else.

84

"Oh, I'm so ashamed."

"Shh, child listen to me for a moment. There's nothing to be ashamed about. You're a real good kid, with many gifted talents.

"When you were conceived certain genes got scrambled and you got more female hormones than male. . If you were born without hands, do you think God would accept you any less.

"No."

"That's right, they are both birth defects and are insignificant in heaven. There are so many prejudice people who need to be educated. They need to recognize how their magnification of petty differences has cheated them. They condemn anything out of the ordinary as being inferior. Some of the greatest artists were gay. If they had let society stifle their creativity we could have lost he beauty of possibly the Sistine Chapel, for example. There have been numerous masterpieces lost due to inferiority complexes that have been created by society. Enjoy who you are because you're someone special." Jesell reached out and gave Peter a friendly hug.

"Enough of this, its hotter then blazes," Jesell said as she raised her tee shirt over her head, taking it off.

"Let's go get some ice cream. Come on," she urged, linking her arm in his. From that moment on they became best friends and Petey became the first apostle.

****

CHAPTER IX

Jesell and Petey were in her bathroom toweling off after a ferocious water balloon fight.

"God Jesell, that wasn't fair. I smell like a French Whore; you know, paybacks are a bitch. What kind of perfume did you put in that balloon anyway?"

"Midnight Ecstasy." She said swatting him with her towel.

"Oh....Oh, you're so lucky I'm a gentleman," he said as he pinned her against the wall with one hand, tickling her profusely with the other.

"Uncle, Uncle, Uncle. Stop please I'm going to pee my pants." They went it the bed room and flung themselves on their backs across the bed.

"I gotta do better, Petey" Jesell began."

"How can you do better---you work almost non-stop now."

"It's just not enough. It's like giving an aspirin to a man to cure his lung cancer."

"I have to get to the heart of the matter. There's just too much anger. I've been modeling some basic concepts in the garage. Do you want to see them."

"Yeah, sure I'd love to."

In the center of the garage was a model of a building surrounded by pleasantly designed homes and apartment buildings. There were pools and parks placed strategically scattered throughout the complexes. Along one edge was a shopping mall, Movie Theater, market, amusement park and water slides. Up against the far wall was a model freeway. It has three lanes filled with tiny little cars spaced at equal distances, alternated on the individual lanes. The space was three car lengths apart.'

"What we have here," Jesell explained, is a small metropolis designed to house a major corporation and its employees. The concept involved is decentralization. Dead lock is reality and that needs to be changed."

"My plan is to somehow convince the government to redirect its spending. All foreign aid, the designing and building of nuclear weapons and Star Wars must stop. "

"Why foreign aid?"

"The aid is not going to the poor; it's lining the pockets of the rich with dollar bills. While we have families not being able to provide nutritious food to their children. Ideally all counties will unite and face these problems together."

"Do you think this government can be turned around?"

"No not really and that is the real problem."

"So how do you propose to sell them on your ideas?"

"Let me explain to you what my ideas actually are; then let's think about that, because I really don't know at this point."

"First, we need decentralization. To start, let's take on hundred major corporations from five of the largest cities and relocate them and their families. The companies would be gone through with a fine-tooth comb, stream lining, re-education, and automating. Education and re-education are major issues and a key for the success of this program. Anyway, this would be enough to complete, proof of design."

"Transportation would be the second issue to be addressed. Freeways should be electromagnetic. Once the car hits the freeway it becomes propelled by an electro-magnetic force. Right now I'm assuming a speed of 200mph. Here, let me show you how it works." Jesell turned on a switch at the end of the table. The car models began moving at a ridiculously fast speed.

"That looks dangerous."

"Why?"

"It's too fast."

"Fifty mph, five hundred mpg—there's no difference. The car is completely controlled in its individual slot. The speed and specification for the area is built into the system. It's programmable; the freeway drives the car. There is no human error involved."

Jesell pushed a button on a computer keyboard. A car from the center lane slid over to the center space of the three car length gap, between two automobiles in the second lane.

"So that's why the cars ad staggered in the different lanes."

"Yeah, for entering or exiting." The car slid to the first lane and was exiting into a platform.

"This platform is for discharging. The outside of the car carries the charges, while the inside is insulated and completely neutral." A car at the entrance platform had already taken the slot left available from the exiting car.

"It will take technology and labor to design and build these devices, therefore, creating jobs. Once the systems are put in place, we will be more than competitive with countries like Japan and China. Our products will become of fraction of their costs and technically advanced."

"The government will be able to amortize their initial investment over twenty years and within six months of completion there will be a substantial profit margin. This will motivate them into taking an overview of the complete picture of the real estate in the United States. So the land can be re-laid out, utilizing all the open spaces efficiently. The objective it to produce the first working model and then strategically introduce the changes across all continents. The world will be one and at peace.

The United States is still one of the leaders in technology. Once the foreign powers see that we've pulled out to the arms race, they're going to sit back and punt, as always, they'll start to copycat our actions, maybe they'll even ask for our help, which we will gladly give. The country will be independently wealthy in a positon to fulfill our obligation with our basic characteristic—generosity. Anyway it will all go something like that."

"Could the government be overthrown?" Petey inquired.

"No, not really, probably not at all. Before that could happen, more than likely, someone would destroy the world. The way I see it, I can use the present system to gain the power I need. I'll need apostles in key positions in congress. I will need enough to gain the controlling vote, but first things first. Are you up to helping me find the next president? Hey! You want the job?"

"I'm only fifteen.

"That was a joke, silly. Besides, I have more fun things in store for you."

****

CHAPTER X

"Over there," Jesell said to Petey, pointing in the direction where a derelict sat on a bench by the beach.

"You're kidding."

"No, I'm not—that's him."

"Why does he look like that?"

"He's living and existing, but he's lost awareness, His emotions reached such a high level that his circuits overloaded temporarily, shorting out his transmitting cells."

"How does something like that happen?"

"At one time he was a well-liked and respected politician, a great leader in his community. About fifteen years ago he had a beautiful wife whom he cherished. They had planned their family and she was six months pregnant. He had the world by the tail on a downhill run. He was young, healthy and had a beautiful wife and a bundle of joy. He was driving home from work, window down, singing along with the radio when he heard sirens and moved over to let an ambulance and several police cars pass. As he wondered what happened, he rounded the corner of his street and got a sickening queasy feeling in his stomach; because as he approached his house he realized they were surrounding it. His neighbor was at the door and tried to restrain him from going in.

"Hey, don't go in there man," he cried. There were tears rolling from his eyes. As he broke from the vice-like grip, the neighbor grabbed at him desperately.

"Johnny, I beg you. Please don't do this to yourself—don't go in there." Unrestrained, he thrust himself through the door. Nancy's mutilated body was lying in a dark pool of blood.

"Looks like homicide," the police chief was saying to his assistant as John entered.

"Oh God – No, No... Nancy, please Nancy, speak to me."

As he reached for her, the sergeant stopped his hand in mid-air.

"I'm sorry sir, but there may be evidence on her person?"

"Yes, yes, oh yes. How? Why? Oh my God, why"

"I was hoping you could tell me that. Come on sir," he continued

"Sit here for a minute. I know this is going to be extremely difficult, but I've got to ask you some questions."

Jesell went on,

"The horrendous nightmare was made worse by the endless questions, detectives, and finger print experts. They invaded his privacy, tore the house inside and out, apologizing over and over again. The first night was endless--- at the funeral he felt like his heart was being ripped from his chest as the first shovelful of earth hit the coffin, he went into shock. He moved, he talked and he functioned unconsciously. Everything he did was in a daze." It's a protection mechanism in the brain, if the realization of what had happened had hit him all at once, it would have been too much and he would have gone off his rocker."

"He looks like he's off his rocker now."

"Well, he is but that happened later. Anyway, eventually he was able to accept the death, and became motivated again and started to build a new life, but there was one thorn in his side. The two young men who were questioned for the murder of his wife were let out on technicalities. He was one hundred percent convinced that they were guilty, so he gave them his own death sentence. He planned their demise methodically. He accepted an assignment which required a business trip. He carried a disguise with him along with a fake I.D. Anyway, he was seen at all the proper places at the right times. During the night he snuck back and carried out his plans. The execution murder was set up to look gang related. So there was never any clues or evidence that linked back to John. Did I tell you that is his name: John?"

"No, but I already gathered that."

"Anyway, his vengeance was satisfied, he thought. The real murderer was discovered with the merchandise and linked DNA, a few months later. Once he was given the news, he picked up a bottle of booze and has never put it down."

"Wow that's sad."

"Yeah." They crept slowly up to John.

"Is he sleeping," Petey asked.

"Passed out is more like it, God he's a mess."

"How are we going to clean him up?"

"I don't know, man he stinks. I don't want to touch him."

"Yuck, me either. I know! Let me run and get some dish soap, then we can roll him onto this blanket and drag him down to the beach, and into the water."

"Sounds good, get a pair of scissors while you are at it."

John was so far gone he did not even flinch as his body hit the water. Jesell and

Petey worked diligently cutting away his clothes. They lathered him up and scrubbed him from head to toe.

"Jesell people are starting to stare at us."

"I'd look too. What we're doing is kind of weird. Hand me that towel we'll make him a lap lap. Come on, stop worrying. This is Venice Beach; these people expect to see almost anything." As John started to recover from his comatose state, he came out fighting.

"I'll get you, you punk sons' of bitches. Come on try me," he shouted as he waved his fist back and forth in mid-air.

Jesell and Petey jumped out of the line of fire. Jesell quietly reached out and grabbed his big toe, as their flesh met, John quieted and he laid back as the alcoholic poison was drawn from his system. Since he had not been sober since he took that first sip, he was transformed back into the dimension and time just before the incident. He started to sob uncontrollably, heart rendering sobs. Jesell reached out and cradled him, rocking back and forth, rubbing his shoulder.

She lamented, "It's alright, it's all right." He opened his eyes slowly and gazed into Jesells beautiful eyes.

"What is happening? Who are you?"

"Shhh, it's not time to talk yet. I want to show you something first." She turned to Petey, "Hey, you want to go on a free ride?"

"Sure," Petey said as he followed Jesell's direction, because he never questioned anything she said or did. He followed – always astonished.

"Okay" she started, "we all join hands, close your eyes and relax I'll do the rest." They slowly started to retreat back into themselves, entering their subconscious. There were little flickering lights shooting back and forth.

"Those are your transmitting cells, John. This is what you were destroying. If you had continued to drink, you would have killed each cell until they were all gone. Once that happens, death is eminent for body and soul. These cells are a link to the internal tunnel that you must cross to enter into eternity. Am I going too fast?

"No, you're not going to fast enough." Peter retorted. "Wow, this is terrific."

"I didn't ask you--your just along for the ride remember? John, are you alright?"

"Sure, I'm fine. Please continue.

"To your right is the wrong direction." Remember once you start to journey on your own, never take that path."

"Why?" Petey questioned, again forgetting he was just along for the ride.

"Someday Petey, I'll tell you about it, but not to complicate matters, first things first. I will just say one thing it is the road of your wisdom and all knowledge you have attain throughout your various lives, during the cleansing process.

As they entered the tunnel Jesell explained,

"This tunnel is the transition into your birth. You're allowed to come to the edge and look at the light, but you must never enter'"

"Why."

"It's forbidden, if you enter most likely you won't have the strength to re-enter your body. Therefore your mission would be incomplete leaving a link to your mortal soul open, creating a compelling force that would anchor your being to a lower energy, with limited power. Only through a natural transition can the cycle be complete that phenomenon has been labeled death."

"Oh gee, let's see now how can I explain. You see we're all a form of energy and these energies are emitted into different plateaus. Once you enter the light, simplistically speaking think if the grid of a vacuum tube, obsolete analogy and complicated go look it up later. Let me just say your energy is charged and there are a series of grids you are at one level on the grid once you have reached a specific level of energy you are drawn higher and would be propelled to the next grid and therefore part of a stronger energy or force. If this transition were to be short circuited. The malfunction would result in a burn out which would lead your energy down the wrong path. I knew this would be too confusing. Just relax, trust and have faith in me and I promise I'll lead you directly down the right path to the ultimate plateau, which has been leveled heaven."

Jesell began to sense Johns growing discomfort.

"Over there is the vision I wish to share with you John." Jesells voice became intense with her excited anticipation.

"Let me explain one thing before you look. What you are about to see is an illusion, there are no solid forms as we know them in heaven." As they passed through a maze of indescribable hues of brilliant colors John focused on a form at the end of the rainbow. He stopped in his tracks and stared as an overwhelming awareness overtook him. There was his beloved Nancy just as beautiful and real as she had been yesterday. John sprang forward thrusting himself into the illusion, when he reached out he realized that Nancy was as far beyond his reach as she had been before he had moved. He became driven like a mad man breaking into a run as he propelled himself forward only to succumb to the image of Nancy's being.

"Oh God," he cried in anguish as he fell to his knees in exhaustion and disillusion. As Jesell reached him she stopped and began to brush back the tears on his contorted grief stricken face. As time passed and John began to regain his composure, Jesell again guided him to the edge of the illusion.

He saw his beloved Nancy staring into a crystal clear pool of water cradling a magnificent and gorgeous infant in her arms. She was humming a soothing lullaby and lovingly caressing the child while gazing into the pool.

"Why that's me, John cried. It's me in the pool as I am now." He realized that they were watching him as he was watching them.

Jesus stood and watched Jesell from afar as she dabbled into the heavenly taboo, he knew time was running out, if he didn't stop her there could be a big price to pay.

"Jesell he demanded what are you up to?" Knowing quite well what she was up to. Startled, Jesell turned and with love in her eyes she said,

"Oh Jesus," she sang joyously," running to greet him.

"About five, eight" with a wink, he affectionately grabbed her by the shoulders.

"You live dangerously my dear."

"I just had to do it this way;" Jesell rushed on as she gulped a little guiltily.

"Save it for your defense if you get caught, you'll need it," he said beginning to sober.

"Seriously Jesell, leave quickly he's busy with the Oplets. Leave before you give him something to think about."

"Will you come thru the tunnel with us?" Jesell asked.

"Sure just make it fast believe me there is no time."

As they turned to run Jesell grabbed John's hand as Jesus grabbed Petey's.

"By the way," Jesell shouted across to Jesus proudly, these are my apostles Petey and John.

"I know I have been watching. Before Jesell could respond, the four were stopped dead in their tracks by a heavenly roar.

"Jesell what in heavens name are you doing?" Christ could hear, I love you father as Jesus gave her a final push through to the end of the tunnel.

Petey and John found themselves floating above the beach. They could see their own bodies, sitting in a circle, hands folded and eyes closed. I sure look terrible John commented to himself.

"You think that's bad Petey" answered squeakily still shaken from their experiences.

"You should have seen yourself before we cleaned you up.

Jesell took the opportunity to exercise her flying skills. She dove to the round at jet propelled speed, reversed thrust and shot straight toward the sun. Feeling at peace with nature and comfort in the familiar freedom, she began doing summer salts and lazy eights all over the sky. She was brought back to reality by a loud blast of thunder as a flash of angry lightening lit the sky.

"A girl can't even have a little fun," Jesell was mumbling under her breath as they re-entered their bodies.

"Huh,"Petey said as they began to open their eyes.

"Oh, nothing, it's just that I'm not supposed to fly while I'm grounded." John turned to Jesell speechless, questions and surprise written in his eyes.

"They've been waiting for you John. The lake you saw was created by Nancy's tears, as she watched you slowly being driven from her.

She has never given up she watches you with faith and hope.

****

CHAPTER XI

"Mom," Jesell called as they entered the condo.

"Mom I'm home."

"In here honey," Martha answered while toweling off her freshly shampooed hair.

"Mom I have a friend I'd like you to meet."

"Okay, just give me a minute," she wound her hair up neatly in a towel and secured her bathrobe, knotting the belt tightly around her waist. She was slightly taken aback when she entered the living room and found a weather beaten man with a rustic completion, wearing only a beach towel.

"Mom John needs some cloths and a place to stay for a while."

"Sure babe no problem. I'll get some of your dad's cloths and you can show John to the spare bed room and Petey," she said waving her hands in front of her.

"I don't know what that smell is, go home and get cleaned up you smell like you've been wallowing in the sewer."

"I knew I shouldn't have eaten those beans for lunch," Petey remarked as he reached for the door ducking to miss the shoe she threw in his direction.

Jesell led John through the artfully decorated home. Warmth radiated from the delicate touch of yesterday's treasures preserved in an array of cozy welcoming comfort. The spare bedroom was equally tranquil, as Jesell took leave of John he sank gratefully back into the comfortable folds of the quilted bed clothing. The last object John focused on before his heavy eyelids succumbed to deep restful sleep, was a picture of Jesell framed in glossy cherry wood. Her twinkling eyes and radiant smile engulfed his weary form, bringing a soothing comfort to his sleep.

As the months passed John's appearance was transformed into one of a handsomely distinguished man. He was well groomed; his eyes shined bright and his cheeks dimpled when he smiled, which he now did quite often.

Jesell and her family devoted one hundred percent of their time nurturing John. They introduced him to the changes of time. Once he began to feel the social and political injustice and strife of current events, he became outraged with conviction which became the catalyst that began to build strength in his newly formed political opinions.

Jesell, Petey and John spent many afternoons strolling amongst the public. They studied the multitudes gathering together a well-rounded portfolio that portrayed many aspects of the complex and diversified personalities that make up today's society.

"Stop for a minute will you." Jesell interrupted their silent vigil as they were strolling through a crowed park. Jesell had some uncanny powers and at times like these she used them. There was a group gathered about 50 feet away from them, attending what appeared to be a company picnic.

"Listen." Jesell instructed them. The voices of several groups became interjected amongst them as they settled themselves on a park bench nearby.

"God damn, Chinks, smell that smell, that shit they are eating smells like a fucking Kotex."

"Look at that chick eating that shit, she has more hair under her arms then my sister's got on her twat."

"If they don't speak the language fucking ship them back to their own country."

"Look at that big fat ass, damn I bet you could fuck the dimples of her cellulite."

"Hey, brother pass the chitterlings, anyway as I was saying, those Mexicans are taking over the neighborhood. It was all black up till last November now there are three houses full of them. It's a God damn shame."

"Hey sister don't eat them greens Shonda made them and I swear girl it's no lie, she picks her nose and dips in the bowl?"

"Hey man there's some white dude looking for you, over there man, there's the ghost, and he's looking for some shit man."

"Look at those white bitches, they're cold, real damn bitches."

Jesell turned off the orientation from the surrounding group

"That's outrageous." Came Petey's first comment.

"It's really quite normal amongst people with no apparent commonality," Jesell answered. If I were to take this group and make them all pink with a universal language, the social disease that stems from being different builds an endless wall. Which builds strength on bigotry and narrow mindedness. It would take some effort to overcome that wall and to create compassion for the unknown, but like I said give them a common color and language it would be like stripping the rainbow of all its colors but one. We need to unite all the differences and introduce them to each other so they can blend together like the colors of the rainbow uniting the color of life."

John spoke softly,

"The unknown can be unfair, the loss of a loved one is un-questionably an outrageous injustice that is beyond any understanding. There is the unbelievable anger that overtakes any and all reality but hate, you have shown, "me" a single chosen individual the end.

The blind injustice or sickness, extreme cruelties and death leave an unquestionable void for anyone, where is the rainbow where is the justice. The end, the beginning the ultimate strength the ultimate love robbed stripped from our being. To prostitute our soul to the belief that the ego mania of a creator that promises endless love and stamps that love out like a disturbing ant is questionable. Oh God, you showed me beyond but there was no touch. You showed me the end to a new beginning, but I could not feel the objects of my affections."

"You John are human as I am human. We must experience all the colors of life we can. I as you will feel extreme sadness when my time comes to leave my earthly existence. This life lends a special gift, without it your cycles would never complete and elevation would be impossible. The only exception being the gifted one born of Down syndrome or the babies too young to reason, for all that heaven is, is theirs. These are the most cherished, the innocent beyond all innocence.

At one point in time the gate to heaven closed by the power of greed. We are lent everything on this earth to leave with nothing, but memories. So to hoard beyond reason earths material treasures is pointless, anyway. God's unselfish sacrifice of his son opened a path back into the gateway of heaven. Now the power that again is causing turmoil in the elements, is selfishness and greed. Heaven is united in one. Only on earth do you walk alone. When we fight and try to control each other we are only fighting ourselves.

This is the reason I'm to be sacrificed, to unite all beings. With endless love he holds a great compassion to save us. The minds of man are becoming confused, the evil powers are disturbing the elements and creating havoc in our hearts and souls. Only through the strength mankind possesses can this energy be fought and conquered in the end."

****

CHAPTER XII

In a few short months John had made enough contacts to get back into the swing of things. Jesell, Petey and John were all working diligently gathering the necessary apostles and disciples to carry out their partially formatted master plan. John's easy going personality, boyish charms and flamboyant personality provided him a free ride back into the heart of politics. He lectured at colleges and at major conventions winning a nomination for the governor's seat. He ran for election with a positive direct, approach offering excellent solutions for the cities ten hottest issues. His victory was a land-side, he walked away with eighty percent of the votes. Once in office John hired professionals to expound on Jessels ideas. As a surprise for her 17th birthday John presented her with a competed package containing their final designs.

Jesell was overwhelmed she felt the concepts superior. The corporate officials and factory facilitates were built underground. The tracks of homes were built above them, in order to utilize the available real estate efficiently. Major thoroughfares and streets were built above and under-ground. There were outstanding plans for educating the young and re-educating the old with obsoleted job skills. The market was analyzed for the best products to manufacture. Economists, efficiency experts, controllers, manager's engineers and top executive brainstormed for a period of six months to put together a major corporate directive.

To say the least, when Jesell reviewed the presentation she was impressed.

"Oh, John you're an absolute genus," she said genuinely complimenting him. She continued to praise and thank him over and over again. When the presentation was concluded and John and Jesell were finally alone, she turned to him and said,

"Let's go find Peter and celebrate."

There was also recognizable changes in Petey, who was now Peter. When Jesell had first contacted him, her touch had straightened out his self-doubt and ingrained in him an acceptance and love for himself, this reinforced any self-doubt he had. He idolized John who had turned into a mentor and a father figure for him. The relationship was perfect for John, Peter filled part of the space in his life left by the void of losing his wife and child. It tickled Jesell to see John's individual personality traits emulated by Peter. Not only did he copycat his traits but he also picked up his style of dress.

Jesell and John went off in search of Peter. They found him in Jesells bedroom reeking of alcohol and flying high on drugs. Jesell's alarm turned to shock as she watched John's reaction. He had Peter pinned to the bed and was plummeting him with hard punches. Jesell was compelled to intervene, but she stopped herself. She knew what he was about to do but resolved not to interfere, for there was a valuable lesson here for both of them to learn. John beat Peter until his energy was spent and he came to his senses. His face was ashen when he at last looked up, he looked incredibly tired and defeated as he silently walked out of the door.

Jesell examined the damage John had done, knowing this was one pain she could not erase. Jesell went to get the first aid kit. The pain signals never penetrated Peters brain, he was just lying on the bed with a blank expression his face. He finally drifted into a deep unconscious sleep.

Before dawn John walked in, he sat down and looked at Jesell forlornly. Jesell broke the silence.

"He's going to be alright John."

"I don't know what came over me, Jesell. I have always been against corporal punishment, when I was a kid I was bigger than the rest of the kids in my class. I was somewhat of a bully, every time I'd beat up some kid, my dad would beat me up. That did not stop me from beating up other kids it just made me meaner.

"Why did you hit Perter?"

"I was mad, I wanted to hurt him like he was hurting me."

"He did not do anything to you, he did it to himself."

"No I don't agree, he did it to a person I love, himself."

"Your right, he triggered a defense mechanism in you. Next time something like this happens act with love, don't fight back."

"Poor kid I didn't even give him the benefit of a doubt. I hope he will understand." Peter stared to stir.

"Oh, my head I feel like I'm dying. Who's here?" He reached out blindly, slightly cracking his eye lids. They opened slowly and painfully.

"I beat you."

"You what?"

"I said I beat you."

Peter became furious, "You God Damn bastard," Peter spat out brokenly.

"What or who gave you the right to touch me?" John looking broken, started to make an ill attempt at an explanation.

"You should understand one thing Peter and that is I love you." Before he could continue, Peter broke in venomously,

"What would you do if you didn't like me cut off my arms and legs? " Peter made an attempt at grabbing John's throat.

"I want to punch your ignorant face in," peter groaned again as the pain overcame him." John reached out to help Peter back on the bed.

"God damn it man, don't touch me." Peter managed to grunt.

"Peter give me a few minutes to explain, if when I'm done you still want to punch me, my face if yours." John said, Peter managed to shout angrily,

"Did you let me explain?"

"No, no Peter I didn't. I made a mistake."

"You're God damn right you made a mistake, I thought you were my friend." Peter continued to lash out.

"I hate you John."

"I love you son, when I saw you last night, I was angry, angry because I love you. I didn't want to lose you like I lost my family. I guess, I saw me in you, when I was hitting you I was somehow hitting myself. You're like my own flesh and blood. If you hurt yourself, you're hurting a person I love and care about very much." They looked at each other, as their eyes met the anger and disbelief slowly started to fade."

"You really love me John?"

"I sure do, Peter."

"Me too," Peter said shyly. Trying to blink back tears.

"Gee," he said as he rudely wiped snot on the back of his hand.

"Me too?" what John started to tease.

"You know man."

"Know what?"

"I love you, there are you happy, I said it."

"Come get up and get dressed you nut." As Peter started to rise, he felt a twinge of pain start to return. As the pain returned so did his vengeance.

"What is the matter man, are you frustrated because you can't screw the object of your affection?"

"You're sick Peter really sick," Peter stopped joking around and began to tell his story.

"This girl was gorgeous, she had knockers out to here, John you would have creamed your jeans looking at her. We were sitting next to each at a party one of the kids was giving from school, we started talking having a real good time; we drank a couple of beers then she pulls these pills out of her purse and offers me one. I wanted to look macho, or something so I took the pill. My intention was to stick it in my pocket when she wasn't looking. I guess I hesitated too long because she took the pill from my hand and put it into my mouth, she grabbed my private parts and I swallowed the pill. We started to drink another beer and I began to feel real funny. It started to sink in how dangerous what I had done was, that was my last rational thought and I got real scared. All I could think of was to find you Jesell. So I went to your house, I crawled up the last few stairs and dragged myself into your room. My head was pulsating in and out, everything was out of shape and crazy looking. The room started to spin it felt like I was growing really big then I would shrink real little. Bright lights filled the room and then everything went black.

Jesell looked at the two kindly, "We are humans and the realization of the wants and needs of our body contradicts the final destiny we will realize with the gift of age and wisdom. Learn to ask for forgiveness and to forgive. The negative affect of guilt will weigh on the dimension of who you are. You do have a spiritual entity that is linked to each life you decide to enter. It's like a spiritual ladder only it is the divine connection to each life, which recognizes the sacred climb to a mystical birth

when we transcendent from one whelm to

another.

****

CHAPTER XIII

There is no end to this story for Jesell still walks amongst us. She is ultimately leaving her foot prints on earth by leading a life of example.

She is the Chinese immigrant who cleans the empty offices at the airport. She is the elderly next door neighbor who smiles from their window watching as the day passes. She is the young boy who plays in the street, kicking a ball to his dad. She is the sick child in the hospital who cries for his mom at night. She is the prisoner who has unjustly been housed from childhood in an adult prison for a crime he did not commit. She is a single mom who works far too long and hard to give the right amount of time to her precious child. She is the Mexican and Afro American couple united in the state of matrimony. She is all around you, just watch for the signs.

As generations pass Jesell and her Apostles leave positive foot prints on the earth. Many generations bringing 1000 years of peace. Not only does DNA affect who a person it is also the evolution of each life in the family chain, from one generation to another.

The miraculous extension is a connection only recognized and achieved from the spirit that has eternal life. Just as a cocoon transitions into a beautiful butterfly so does our soul transition into a brilliant light.

For all is lost and all is gained when we returned to hence we came. Freewill gives us the ability to disrupt the natural flow from one birth to the next. The realization that the journey is to begin and goes through phases, ultimately achieving the grace and glory that is ours.

PEACE, FORGIVENESS, FAITH, HOPE, CHARITY AND LOVE

****

ABOUT THE AUTHOR

Colleen Khalfia, is a retired Process Engineer who worked in her field for over 50 years and is seen here with her grandson. While cleaning the storage area of her home she came upon a book written by her 28 years ago. The pages were brittle and decomposing, she could either throw it away or retype it for preservation, and she decided to resurrect the project so here it is, read it at your own discretion.

She wants to thank her son and daughter who have been her inspiration as she watches them grow into the amazing adults they are from the amazing children they were. She still sees in the twinkle of their eyes,the babies she once held and caressed.

We all experience heaven when we hold a child and look into their eyes the first time.